MY ALABASTER BOX...

POETRY, PROSE, AND PRAYER

VOLUME I

CATHERINE ELAINE MCPHERSON

ISBN 978-1-64416-448-8 (paperback)
ISBN 978-1-64492-108-1 (hardcover)
ISBN 978-1-64416-449-5 (digital)

Christian Faith Publishing, Inc.
832 Park Avenue
Meadville, PA 16335
www.christianfaithpublishing.com

Printed in the United States of America

"MY ALABASTER BOX," IS DEDICATED TO
THE SAVIOR OF THE WORLD
THE LORD OF LORDS
AND
KING OF KINGS
THE ONLY BEGOTTEN SON OF GOD
JESUS CHRIST
YESHUA HA'MASHIACH
AMEN.

CONTENTS

PREFACE

WORDS ARE IMPORTANT. SO important that mothers rejoice when their offspring utters their first word, recording it in that all too soon to be neglected baby book. So important that the grieving chisel words on granite headstones of their newly departed loved ones. Words beckon us to breakfast in the morning and tuck us into bed at night. Life, as we experience it on earth, begins and ends with words.

The Bible has a lot to say about words: "Life and death is in the power of the tongue and he that loves it shall eat the fruit of thereof" "Let your 'Yes' be 'Yes,' and your 'No' be 'No.'" "By your words you are justified and by your words you are condemned" "Don't you know that you shall give account of every idol word you speak on the day of judgment?" And those verses are just a few. There is enough about *words* in the Bible to write a book. Perhaps, someday, I shall. But that book is not this one. This book is about the words, of my heart. It is the written rhyme and rhythm of life experiences as processed through poetry, prose, and prayer.

Fortunately for me, my parents gave their children the gift of a Christian worldview. They offered us Jesus and encouraged us to grow in faith. I accepted. So the entries within the covers of this volume are written from the basis of biblical truth as I understand it. Processing life is just that, a process, and that process is so much more productive if we embrace the Giver of Life as our Guide.

It is my prayer that you, the reader, will use these humble insights to kick-start your own dialogue with the One who speaks. The format is a meditation for each day of the month, but there is

7

also a topical table of contents and a scriptural index. I hope, above all, that you receive a blessing and a word of encouragement as you read the words from *My Alabaster Box*. Amen.

INTRODUCTION

WHAT SHE HAD WAS an alabaster box.

What she did not have was a very good reputation.

What she had was a year's salaries worth of precious perfume, exquisite oil reserved for that proverbial *rainy day.*

What she did not have was an invitation to the dinner party being given by Simon the Pharisee in honor of the still undeclared Messiah of Israel.

What she did have was an overwhelming gratitude for the touch of His grace on her totally broken life—and a passion to give back to the One that stooped to lift her up.

What she did not have was an easy entrance into the presence of Jesus Christ the God-man that was reclining for a meal with the religious leaders of the nation.

What she did have was courage.

Stepping inside the open door, she moved quickly and purposefully. With one fluid movement, she both broke the seal on the marble vase and poured its perfume as an anointing on the precious head of God.

And before she could be reprimanded, the redolence of her riches ricocheted off the walls of the small room riveting the eyes of the religious on her sacrifice. Before the indignant could intervene, she was weeping over the feet of her Savior; her tears mingling with the oil to produce the holy anointing ointment of adoration.

The Pharisees were appalled.

The Lord was pleased.

What she had given was the hidden wealth of her secret life. What she received was the rewarding words from her Redeemer—wonderful words that rebuked her ridiculers and reinforced her inheritance as a child of the King. Please read on:

> Now when the Pharisee who had invited Him saw this, he said to himself, "If this man were a prophet He would know who and what sort of person this woman is who is touching Him, that she is a sinner."
>
> And Jesus answered him, "Simon, I have something to say to you." And he replied, "Say it, Teacher."
>
> "A moneylender had two debtors: one owed five hundred denarii, and the other fifty.
>
> When they were unable to repay, he graciously forgave them both. So which of them will love him more?"
>
> Simon answered and said, "I suppose the one whom he forgave more." And He said to him, "You have judged correctly."
>
> Turning toward the woman, He said to Simon, "Do you see this woman? I entered your house; you gave Me no water for My feet, but she has wet My feet with her tears and wiped them with her hair.
>
> You gave Me no kiss; but she, since the time I came in, has not ceased to kiss My feet.
>
> You did not anoint My head with oil, but she anointed My feet with perfume.
>
> For this reason I say to you, her sins, which are many, have been forgiven, for she loved much; but he who is forgiven little, loves little."
>
> Then He said to her, "Your sins have been forgiven."

Those who were reclining at the table with Him began to say to themselves, "Who is this man who even forgives sins?"

And He said to the woman, "Your faith has saved you; go in peace. (Luke 7:39–50 NASB)

In the same attitude of gratitude and grace, as an abandoned adorer of the Almighty, do I, hereby, break my own *alabaster box.* May my word offerings of poetry, prose, and prayer be a powerful perfume that carries you into His presence.

Amen.

COURAGE 1

I would rather face
The gale wind force
Struggling hard against the waves
Than row the placid
Ocean surface, day
After endless day

I would rather crash
Against the rocks, fighting
Hard against the pain
Than live in quiet solitude
Where nothing
Is to gain

I would rather rail
Into the tempest
Challenging the storm
Than hide in so called
Safety, embracing nothing
But the norm

I would rather sail
Beyond what is seen
Drawing faith from courage sown
Than stand with those
Who never move for
Fear of the unknown

Blow me wind
Oh, Wind of God
Across the ocean of your grace
Where Leviathan
Stands waiting for
The Victor's winning pace

And even though
I'm weak, I choose
The harder course
For I have found
Within me
My Lord God
The Greater Force.

....The Lord is my strength and my defense; He
has become my salvation.—King David
Psalm 118:14

...I can do all things through Christ who
strengthens me.—The Apostle Paul
Philippians 4:13

FOLLOWING CHRIST IS FOR the courageous! He continually calls
us "out of the boat," "up the mountain," and "onto the raging waves."
The easy life is not the way of the Cross. This obedient life, that
mirrors the life of Christ, is a blessed life that teaches us to embrace
trials as avenues of victory. We are not alone in this challenge, for it
is in Christ that we find courage beyond our cowardice, strength in
our self-absorption, and faith that defies our fears. He is not looking
for excuses for why we did not, but hearts yielded beyond the "whys"
of life's traumas. No, my fellow pilgrim, what we are called to is not

easy, but it is eternally worth the struggle to step out of the boat, climb up the mountain, and walk on the water. He is with us. Amen.

Prayer:

Father in heaven,
I thank You, that You have called my name. Fill me with
Your Holy Spirit that I may have the strength and
courage to complete the course. Place within my heart
Your heavenly directives for each day and each hour.
May I always desire that which stretches my faith and
fills me with the wonder of Your provision.
In the name of Jesus the Courageous,
Amen.

My Personal Reflections

_____
_____
_____
_____
_____
_____
_____

HOPE

2

I was lost, You gave me direction
I was afraid, You gave me courage
I was weak, You gave me strength
I had no hope, You gave me Yours
I was blind, You gave me sight
I was naked, You gave me robes of righteousness
I was hungry, You gave me the bread of heaven
I was thirsty, You gave me drink from the Rock of Ages
I was cold, You gave me love that warmed my soul
I had no home, You gave me paths to dwell in
I was lonely, You gave me friendship that fostered my faith
I was sinking deep in sin, You gave Your life that lifted me to eternity
I was and I am forever grateful....

...And He is The One who is before all, and all
things exist by Him.—The Apostle Paul
Colossians 1:17

...For in Him, we live and move and have
our being.—The Apostle Paul
Acts 17:28

THE WORD "EPIPHANY" IS defined as "a sudden realization or appearance of God." It came to me as a mighty rushing wind that blew away the spirit of all-hope-lost. So strong the breath of the Lord that chased away the chaff from the threshing floor of my life that it seemed self was a mere shell of what I had been. What remained was ripe for the Holy Spirit to continue to crush for the purpose of making fine flour: the kind that is produced for making the most expensive bread. This bread can then be used to feed those who are hungry, for those whom nothing has been prepared. So has been my life; broken, bruised, gathered, refined, remade, and cast upon the waters. In His hands nothing is wasted. It is enough. Amen.

Prayer:

Father in heaven,
Nothing is impossible with You for You are
the Lord, the God of all flesh.
Thank You for finding me when I was so lost
and seeing me as worthy of Your love.
You have given all things so that those who believe
may live forever in Your holy presence.
Thank You for your heart of devotion to the prisoners of this earth.
I pray in the name of Jesus Your Son,
Amen.

My Personal Reflections

_____

_____

_____

_____

_____

_____

_____

STEADFASTNESS 3

I could have loved you more
My words too few were kind
Even though I smiled a smile
Frustration plagued my mind

I wanted only good for you
A life without such pain
I offered prayers but faith
Remained a prize I could not gain

I wish I had a second chance
Would life repeat its beat?
Or would I conquer a selfish heart
And render pride's defeat?

You are not here, you've gone ahead
Your faith has become now sight
And e'er I wish you back to earth
I have no thought or right

To those who care for ailing kin
To those whose hands are tired
Reach softly to that wounded soul
Before the funeral bier

Speak the simple syllables
We all long now to hear

Push regret beyond your reach
With compassion and a tear

It only costs denial
That song of self-defense
To reassure that special one
Of love's true recompense

...So then, whenever we have an opportunity, let us
do good to all people, and especially to those who
belong to the family of faith.—The Apostle Paul
Galatians 6:10

...Love is patient, love is kind...love bears all things believes
all things, endures all things.—The Apostle Paul
I Corinthians 13:4, 7

EIGHTY-NINE YEARS IS CONSIDERED a long time to live and an indication of a blessing from the Lord according to Psalm 91:16, "The Lord will satisfy you with long life." My mother's years were many, but if asked about her life, she would often respond as the patriarch Jacob when Pharaoh asked him about the length of his days: "Few and hard have been the days of the years of my life." (Gen 47:7–10) Her answer was framed by many days filled with physical pain and mental anguish. Consequently, the blessing of life became too much for her to embrace.

I often tried to pull her from the slough of despondency, but the mire seemed too thick. Occasionally, however, success would come balanced on a single beam of enlightened prayer that broke through the dark storm clouds of unbelief. But, alas, it was unsustainable. My own inability to gain the higher ground saddens me to this day. Regardless, I am greatly comforted in knowing that when we meet again, all her pain, and mine as well, will have been absorbed in the awesome beauty of heaven's divine order. I am very thankful. Amen.

Prayer:

Father in heaven,
Tenderize our hearts with the needs of the chronically ill.
Blow away the temptation to be indifferent to constant
suffering. Let us not run away from pain or
refuse to look to the needs of the hurting.
Give us a heart that receives an assignment
of consolation and comfort.
In the name of Your suffering Savior, Jesus,
Amen.

My Personal Reflections

_____
_____
_____
_____
_____
_____
_____

HEAVEN
4

A vision of my mother, Jo Ann Shelton McCabe, the day after she left earth for heaven.

I saw her standing
      Silently just beyond the veil
In white and lace, so lovely
      With flowers blue and pale

She turned to walk
      Those golden streets
Her steps both strong and light
      Flowing from a rhythm
That gave music song and sight

She waved at me with perfect hands
      No longer gnarled and bent
A happy smile now graced her lips
      With kisses heaven sent

I saw her kneeling at the throne
      With joy surrounding all
And beauty flowed encompassing
      The worshippers sweet call

I saw her sweetly swaying
      Just beyond the veil

Encouraging us to finish
    Strong with Jesus at the sail

She's gone ahead
She's entered in
Eternity she's claimed
Our Lord has led
Her safely home
And every weakness tamed.
Amen.

...He will swallow up death forever. The Sovereign LORD will wipe away the tears from all faces; he will remove his people's disgrace from all the earth. The Lord has spoken.—The Prophet Isaiah
Isaiah 25:8

...And all the angels were standing around the throne and around the elders and the four living creatures and they fell on their faces before the throne and worshipped God, saying, "Amen, blessing and glory and wisdom and thanksgiving and honor and power and might, be to our God, forever and ever. Amen."—John the Apostle
Rev. 7:11–12

IN MY SIX DECADES on earth, I have yet to meet anyone that desires to go anyplace but heaven when they die. Perhaps it is that God-shaped hole in our heart that yearns for completion and draws us toward our heavenly home. The writer of the book of Ecclesiastes puts it this way: "He has made everything beautiful in its time. He has also set eternity in the human heart." (Ecclesiastes 3:11)

So if heaven is our true home how then do we arrive safely there? Jesus the Christ made it very plain: "I am the way, the truth and the life, no one comes to the Father but through me." (John 14:6)

Come we must with belief in our hearts and confession on our tongues: "I tell you the truth, those who listen to my message and believe in God who sent me have eternal life. They will never be condemned for their sins, but they have already passed from death unto life." —Jesus Christ. (John 5:24) And in the book of Romans, the Tenth Chapter and Ninth Verse, it is stated: "...If you confess with your mouth the Lord Jesus and believe in your heart that God has raised Him from the dead, you shall be saved. For with the heart one believes unto righteousness, and with the mouth confession is made unto salvation." Mom would tell you, "Don't miss heaven!"

Amen.

Prayer:

Heavenly Father,
Thank You for making the way to reconcile all mankind
through the blood of Your only begotten Son, Jesus Christ.
Thank you that heaven awaits all those that
put their trust in the finished
works of Calvary that remits our sins and reconciles us to You.
We are eternally grateful that You have promised that all
that call upon the name of the Lord shall be saved.
In the name of the One Who brings salvation, Jesus Christ,
Amen.

My Personal Reflections

_____
_____
_____
_____
_____
_____
_____

Written at the death of my first cousin Roger.

Where are you today
        Dear Roger?
I ask, for I do not know

Are you resting in peace
        With the Father
Or somewhere far below?

Where are you standing
        Now brother
I wish I could be sure

Are you comforted by
        The Savior?
By the promise that shall endure?

Forgive me for
        Never asking
Was it because I did not care?

Or living life
        That snared me
With topics much more fair?

MY ALABASTER BOX...

So where is Roger
      Today friends?
We cannot know his heart

But if he stepped
      Toward Jesus
We know Father did His part

We all will travel
      The same way
Ignorance we cannot claim

We'll give account
      Of life given
Times of joy and times of shame

Jesus our Savior
      Is waiting
His arms are open wide

He receives us
      As weary travelers
By His grace we shall abide

Let us turn our hearts
      Toward heaven
Earth is passing away

The Father is drawing us
      Back to Himself
Receive Him as I pray

"Forgive us all
      We ask You
We open our hearts today

25

Believing our sins
Are Forgiven
Through Jesus Your chosen way."

Amen

...All that call upon the name of the Lord
shall be saved.—The Apostle Paul
Romans 10:13

...I am not ashamed of the Gospel of Christ
for it is the power of God unto
salvation to the Jew first and also the Greek.—The Apostle Paul
Romans 1:16

THE GRIM REAPER DOES not usually send a calling card. He arrives unannounced like a thief in the night. So it was with my cousin Roger. One day he was with us, the next day he was not. It was Benjamin Franklin who reminded us that there are only two things certain in life: death and taxes. Taxes we are able to take care of as we will, death not so much.

When I turned 60 years of age, I began getting unsolicited advertisements in my mailbox of preplanned funeral arrangements. Really? Is that the "significant" age in which I am suddenly expected to focus on my own demise? I was somewhat put off and huffy as I rather haughtily threw the unwelcomed solicitations in the garbage.

Then, I received the phone call informing me that Roger had passed. Roger, my cousin that was several years younger than myself. His death arrested me. Even though I was confident in my relationship with Jesus, I was not confident in his. The death angel came for Roger before I was ready. Was Roger ready, "Solo Dios sabe."

Roger's death brought a fresh awareness of eternity. My heart was tenderized to the plight of those living and dying without the

Lord. I was reminded that it is not the Lord's desire that any should perish but all should come to the acknowledgement of the truth.

Prayer:

Father in heaven,
May we think about eternity before we find ourselves separated
from earth and catapulted into the next dimension by death.
May we secure our souls by not just a casual
confession of Christ, but by living a life that mirrors
true faith and obedience to the heavenly call.
In the name of the One who justifies us, Jesus the Christ,
Amen.

My Personal Reflections

_____
_____
_____
_____
_____
_____
_____

No other passion but the cross
No other pain but personal loss
No compromise to the heavenly call
No compulsion that desires me to fall
No other goal but to please the King
No other song but His praises to sing
No other solution for the world's demise
No other salvation for the soul's one sigh
My life, my death
The cross, my cross
In giving my all
I gain what I've lost

…And he said to them all, If any man will come after me, let him deny himself, and take up his cross and follow me.—Jesus Christ
Luke 9:23

…He is no fool who gives what he cannot keep to gain what he cannot lose.—Jim Elliot, martyred missionary to the Huaorani people of Ecuador

Total surrender. Just what might that look like for the average American Christian?
Sunday morning worship service: 1–2 hours
Wednesday evening prayer or Bible study: 1–2 hours

Working a summer Vacation Bible School: maybe
Community Outreach: too many conflicts
Morning prayer and devotionals: 5-minute plan or 15-minute plan
Saying "grace" over each meal: usually
Saying bedtime prayers if you have children: possibly
Tithing: most don't, "not New Testament"
Giving above the tithe: not normal
Abstaining from alcohol: not necessary
Abstaining from R rated movies and above: not required
Viewing pornography: very possible, "it's everywhere"
Same-sex marriage: needed for inclusion
Staying faithful to the wife of ones youth: passé
Going on mission trips to preach the gospel: only for the select few
Taking care of the orphan and widow: may send money at Christmas
Laying hands on the sick: passed away
Casting out demons: refer to mental health agency
Denying self: God only wants the best for me
Take up your cross: I put up with my spouse
Follow Jesus: Yes, heaven is mine!
I Surrender All: an old hymn
Amen.

Prayer:

Father in heaven,
May we not love in word only, but in truth and deed.
Please bring conviction to attitudes and actions that are
neither biblical nor are they pleasing in Your sight.
We desire to do Your will apart from the influences of our culture
and typical "church" examples. Have Your way in our lives.
In the strong and sacrificial name of Jesus,
Amen.

CATHERINE ELAINE McPHERSON

My Personal Reflections

_____
_____
_____
_____
_____
_____
_____

SPIRITUAL WARFARE 7

I thank you my Father
My Savior My Lord
For calling me forth
For anointing my sword

For mountains to climb and
Cold rivers to cross
For battles to fight and
To stand without loss

Positioned in peace
Emboldened by love
Strengthened by courage
That's forged from above

Millions are waiting
To hear the good news
Sitting in darkness
With no path to choose

Lifting the banner
I press on in the fight
To herald His victory
And bring forth the light

CATHERINE ELAINE McPHERSON

Our enemies present
But under our feet
The blood of the Lamb
Demanding defeat

Not looking backward
I battle on in the fray
Engaging the minions
A winning display

Undaunted by demons
Nor thoughts of dis'ray
Looking now upward
For that heavn'ly way

Standing strong in the battle
Increasing the field
Establishing good
Refusing to yield

The challenge still rings out
To those that will hear
And those that respond will
Have nothing to fear

"Gird up your loins and
Follow closely My lead
Put on your armor
And mount now your steed

There's nothing to lose
And heaven to gain
Conq'ring evil by
My crimson red stain

Heralding justice
And refusing to bow
Showing My passion
With purpose for now."

...Thou therefore endure hardness as a good
soldier of Jesus Christ. No man
that wars entangles himself with the affairs of this life; that he may
please him who hath chosen him to be a soldier.—The Apostle Paul
2 Timothy 2:4

...Now thanks be unto God, which always causes us to
triumph in Christ, and makes manifest the savor of his
knowledge by us in every place.—The Apostle Paul
2 Corinthians 2:14

IN THE POLITICALLY CORRECT society in which we live, it is easy
to forget the politically incorrect statements Jesus made to his dis-
ciples. Perhaps, we really have not forgotten them, but certainly we
justify not affiliating ourselves with such "extremism." After all, who
will embrace a Jesus that suggests we leave mother and father and
lands and homes and occupations for the gospel's sake? (Matt. 19:29)
And who among us seeks a ministry in such things as casting out dev-
ils and healing lepers? (Matt. 10:8) Isn't it easier to say "no" to such
instructions if we view ourselves as mere adherents to a "faith" rather
than soldiers in the army of God? Which one are you? The Lord is
still looking for a "few good men." Perhaps we should remember that
the world was turned upside down by only twelve. (Acts 17:6) Amen.

Prayer:

Our Father,
Who art in heaven, hallowed be thy name.
Increase our faith to obey the words of Christ as they
are written, as they are impressed upon our hearts, and
as Your Holy Spirit whispers them to our souls.
In the perfect name of Jesus,
Amen.

My Personal Reflections

_____
_____
_____
_____
_____
_____
_____

THE KINGDOM 8

The tiny seed
Unless it dies
Alone and solitary
It must abide—

⊱✦⊰

…Very truly I tell you, unless a kernel of wheat falls to
the ground and dies, it remains only a single seed. But
if it dies, it produces many seeds.—Jesus Christ
John 12:24

…The kingdom of God is like a man who casts seed into the
ground; and should sleep, and rise night and day, and the seed
should spring and grow up, and he knows not how.—Jesus Christ
Mark 4:26

IT SEEMS TO ME rather backward, the kingdom of heaven. Of
course, that is looking from the outside in. For instance, if we want
to be great, we must be the servants of all. If we want to be first we
have to be last. It is the meek that will inherit the earth not the "mov-
ers and the shakers." Strange isn't it?

Jesus was rather "up front" with those that sought His kingdom,
however. So much so that he informed a wealthy, young, politician
that if he wanted to follow him, he must first sell all his possessions
and give them to the poor. That really was not what the privileged

seeker was expecting; therefore, he left the presence of the God-man dejectedly sad.

Jesus informed his often confused disciples that if they sought to save their lives they would lose them And if they gave their lives away for the Gospel's sake they would truly save them. It is the truth of losing self in His service that gains for us eternal rewards. Thus, the seed buried and invisible to the world someday becomes the mighty oak. (John 12:24) Amen.

Prayer:

Father in heaven,
We praise You for Your perfection. We thank You that Your ways are higher than our ways, and that they are past finding out. It is by faith that we live out Your life instructions. Enable us by Your perfect Holy Spirit to work out our salvation in harmony with the true gospel that bids us come and die. We pray in the name of Your true servant, Jesus Christ, Amen.

My Personal Reflections

_____
_____
_____
_____
_____
_____
_____

FORGIVENESS 9

How sharp the
blade that
doth betray
A heart so easily flayed

And what the
source of
such abuse
The silent case is made.

❦

...The tongue also is a fire, a world of evil among the parts
of the body, it sets the whole course of one's life on fire,
and is itself set on fire by hell.—James the Apostle
James 3:6

...Forgive us our trespasses as we forgive those
who trespass against us.—Jesus Christ.
Matthew 6:12

HAVE YOU NOTICED THAT we sometimes come into contact
with the aftermath of other people's pain? We may be enjoying life,
just minding our own business, when the unfiltered verbiage of a
wounded heart winds up wiping out the goodness of the moment;
hurt people, hurt people. And often it doesn't take much: a sarcastic
comment, a muffled critique of your coiffure, or a rude response to a
well meant conversation starter. It happens.

More importantly, on a deeper level, the unkind words of those closest to us become more than just a momentary downer. Certain syllables seem to sear our hearts whether intentional or unintentional. Those cutting comments fester easily if not quickly contained by forgiveness tendered whether asked for or not. Forgiveness benefits the forgiver more than the "forgivee."

It has been said that withholding forgiveness is like drinking poison and expecting it to kill the one who offended us. We really do become the recipient of our own recalcitrance. We must keep short accounts and allow the oil of the Holy Spirit to mollify every wound and heal every broken heart. Jesus showed us the way: "Father forgive them for they know not what they do." May His example be our response. Amen.

Prayer:

My Father in heaven,
I choose to freely forgive all those who have wounded me
with their unkind words. Even those who have not asked me
to forgive them, especially those Lord. By releasing them and
absolving them, I ask that their hearts are not bound by my
unforgiveness but freed to receive the ministry of the Holy Spirit.
I pray this in the name of the forgiving Jesus,
Amen.

My Personal Reflections

_____

_____

_____

_____

_____

_____

_____

OBEDIENCE

10

I sang a song to the stars last night
       And spoke softly to the moon
I listened hard for their response
       A sonnet or a tune…

Instead the voice that crossed my heart
       Replied to my soulish sigh
Not from the heavenly lighted orb
       But from the Creator of the sky

"Why do you long for what is not yours
       And cry for what will never be?
It only clouds your future hopes
       And confuses what you see

Listen child to My heart's song
       For it is pure and it is true
A poem so perfectly ascribed
       For the one and only you"

Even though His words were soft
       I shuddered at their weight
I knew in honesty He wrote
       Upon my heart His fate

I would never more return
       To embrace the desert moon

Nor sing the song my soul
> Composed beneath the summer lune

But, perhaps, eternity
> Will call my soul to rest
And I will understand the plan
> The struggle and the test.

> …What I do you know not now; but you
> shall know hereafter—Jesus Christ
> John 13:7

> …The mind of man plans his way, but the LORD
> directs his steps.—King Solomon Proverbs 16:9

I THOUGHT I HAD "arrived." After years of doing short term mission work, we were finally on the mission field "full time." Even though we were technically "home missionaries" it didn't feel that way. The culture on the Texas border is much more Mexican than Anglo. Our son who has lived there for 18 years refers to it with a grin as "North Mexico." It didn't matter the name assigned, I was elated. Cross cultural ministry was perfect in my book. I loved the Spanish language, the dark eyes and black hair. I loved the tortillas, the paletas, the sopas and frijoles.

We were partnering with an established church in South Texas to help the Mexican refugees that were flooding over the border. They had come to escape the violent drug cartels that were terrorizing the general population. We had "found" our place…or so I thought.

Living in a FEMA trailer, east of Laredo, we had many opportunities to feed the hungry, cloth the naked and offer a drink of cold water in the name of Jesus. It was a challenge that I embraced and relished.

But all was not well in Dodge City. The further we got into our "mission" of 2 ½ years, the more the Lord showed us we were not in the right place. He showed, I resisted. He was faithful to reveal, but I was neglectful to heed. I wanted this adventure to work with all my heart. Maybe that was the issue. Instead of just the overflow of loving the Lord with all my heart, all my mind, all my soul and all my strength, I was in love with the "ministry." Ouch.

So, one week we were there helping teams of short term missionaries to touch broken lives in the desert and the next week we were back on secluded Redbud Lane in rural southeastern Oklahoma; culture shock in reverse. It took me several months to "accept" the Lord's decision to move us back home. I cried a lot. I rehearsed my failures. I repented. I bargained to return. I rocked silently in the decades-worn maple rocker.

In the end, or should I say in "the beginning again," the Lord's mercy prevailed. Thankfulness started as a small stream from my broken heart and finally, like a fountain, it baptized my soul in hope and purpose. Lesson learned: "A man's heart plans his way, but the Lord directs his steps." And "as for the Lord, all His ways are perfect." Amen.

Prayer:

Father in heaven,
Life is too short to maneuver without Your blessing and direction.
Thank You that You are always watching over us to get us to
the right place at the right time. We bless Your purposeful
hand that always causes us to triumph in Christ Jesus.
For it is written that You know the plans You have for us, plans for
good and not evil to give us a future and a hope, an expected end.
Blessing Your goodness in the name of our
good shepherd, Jesus Christ,
Amen.

My Personal Reflections

_____

_____

_____

_____

_____

_____

_____

TEMPTATION 11

The desert rose
Blooms for an hour
Unseen, untouched, unknown
Until a Pilgrim
Passes by
With God's own wind is blown

At first glance
There is no pull
No touching of the stem
A casual nod
To recognize
The beauty deep within

The Pilgrim stops
And stoops to see
The smallish petals bend
And suddenly in
Full desire
Becomes its closest kin

We are alike
My desert friend
We both have thorns that rend
Our brokenness
Attracts the stares
Of those that would not bend

Our lives have touched eternity
Our souls a perfect blend
But Pilgrim
Stands and starts away
The road before him sends

A message to
His wandering heart
Touch not the rose, it's sin
How could it be
The fragrance bids
One's heart to enter in

Just for a moment
Lost in time
It's tenderness to lend
One counts the cost and steps away
Although the loss a friend
Means cherishing eternity
The life that cannot end.

...And what shall a man give in exchange for his soul?—Jesus Christ
Mark 8:37

...God cannot be tempted with evil neither tempts he any
man, but every man is tempted when he is drawn away
by his own lust and enticed...—The Apostle James
James 1:13

MATURITY IS ONE OF the only friends we have that will deny satisfaction to our inner self. It's his voice that will warn against impulse and compulsion. The older we become, and with practiced obedience, maturity will always weigh in on the side of sanity. Not that everyone that's of eldership is wise. There is a true saying my mother used to parrot: "There's no fool like an old fool." But if we allow reason to touch our heart, right behavior is in reach and victory is calling our name. We must be vigilant not to throw away the very plan of the Lord for the beauty of the alluring and the expedient. Amen.

Prayer:

Our Father in heaven,
Lead us not into temptation and deliver us from evil.
Teach us Your ways that we may know Thee.
Empower us by Your Spirit to overcome the
world, the flesh, and the devil.
In the name of your sinless Son, Jesus,
Amen.

My Personal Reflections

_____
_____
_____
_____
_____
_____
_____

*H*OPE

12

So what happens
When dreams
Turn to dust
And hope takes a holiday?

When plans perceived
Become but
Distant thoughts—

And all accumulated
Desire drains
From the broken heart

Is there a remedy?
A potion powerful
Enough to pacify the pain?

Does it even matter?
"Out, out, brief candle."

And who will notice?
Just another flickering light
Swallowed by the silent storm?
What trespassing specter manipulates the soul?

The spirit moans from sorrow
But truth seeks a higher
Plain

That only the Spirit Holy
From the breath of God
Contains
and
Speaks to life the saddened
Soul and brings
To hope again.

...Why so downcast, Oh my soul, and why
are you disquieted within me?
Put your hope in God: for I will yet praise him,
who is the health of my countenance,
and my God.—King David
Psalm 43:5

...We are hard pressed on every side, but
not crushed; perplexed, but not in
despair; persecuted, but not abandoned; struck
down, but not destroyed.—The Apostle Paul
2 Corinthians 4:9

IT IS DARK THE shadow of hopelessness. Surprisingly subtle he finds avenues of ministry even in the blessings of the Lord. When we neglect to praise Him in every situation, the advantage goes to the enemy. What the Lord intends to turn to good becomes stuck in the miry clay of an ungrateful heart.

Self-pity accompanies such a short-sighted out look. And the victim-mentality slips into our thoughts like a thief in the night.

Unknowingly the accusations against injustices perceived become a finger pointing at the veracity of the goodness of Yahweh.

It is the work of the deceiver.

The always-effective-antidote: praise! Job, the Jewish patriarch, was well acquainted with adversity. In one day he lost his ten children, all his flocks, herds and servants. His amazing response is as follows:

"Naked I came from my mother's womb and naked shall I return there. The Lord gave and the Lord has taken away. Blessed be the Name of the Lord…and though he slay me yet will I praise him."

Let us do no less.
Choose to praise.
And darkness flees.
Amen.

Prayer:

Father in heaven,
Let Your high praises always be on our lips. Forgive us when
we have chosen to dwell in the darkness of despondency
instead of fellowshipping around the fire of faith.
Create in us clean hearts and take not thy Holy Spirit from us.
Always praying in the name of Your Son,
Jesus Christ,
Amen.

My Personal Reflections

_____
_____
_____
_____
_____
_____
_____

ENCOURAGEMENT 13

Every tear that falls
          The master saves
Every sigh that's whispered
          A journey paves
Every groan withheld
          Becomes a prayer
Every cry released
          Builds a heavenly stair

So near is His hand
          So close to our cause
No demon can reckon
          Or hasten our loss
No weapon can challenge
          Or counter His heart
No circumstance formed
          Can destroy our life's part

Jesus our Savior
          Has endured for us all
We have only to stand
          To answer the call
Never alone He surrounds
          Us with love
He emboldens with peace
          And power from above

...He keeps all our tears in a bottle...—King David
Psalms 56:8

...All things work together for good to those
that love the Lord and are the called
according to His purpose.—The Apostle Paul
Romans 8:28

NOTHING IS WASTED IN the Lord's economy. Even the scraps of bread that were picked up from that huge picnic in which Jesus fed the 5000 with two fish and five loaves of bread were saved. In fact, there were so many "left overs" that they filled twelve baskets full. That's a lot of bits and pieces. Think about it, if the Lord was concerned that the bread crumbs be saved don't you think he cares much more about the broken pieces of our hearts?

His redemption is so much more than just a ticket to heaven; so exceedingly more than the promise of an eternal mansion beyond the celestial sea. The relationship we have with the Father encompasses making sense of all the failures and detours of our lives. Perhaps, not putting everything in logical cubes of complete comprehension, but a relinquishment into the hands of the One that makes all things new. Understanding that He knows and cares somehow comforts and converts the misery into mercy. Amen.

Prayer:

Our Father in heaven,
How great and wonderful You are. How intimately acquainted
You are with all our ways. Thank You for taking all the torn pieces
of our lives and fashioning them into a garment of praise. You are
both willing and able, and we are both humbled and grateful.
Praying in the name of Jesus who makes all things new,
Amen.

My Personal Reflections

_____

_____

_____

_____

_____

_____

_____

SANCTIFICATION 14

When we come to the very end of ourselves,
    We realize that in Him there is a beginning
        Not known before

When we recognize we are nothing apart from Him
    We understand in Him we
        Are everything

Not until all is lost are we able to
    Find ourselves in Him

Not until darkness totally prevails
    Do we embrace the hope
        That is His light personified

Only when sin strips us naked are
    We able to wrap ourselves in
        His robes of righteousness

Only when the sting of death
    Pulsates through our mortal
    Bodies are we finally able
        To be re-born into
            Everlasting life

Then and only then are we vessels
    Meet for His service

Then and only then do we fully appreciate
        The total sacrifice of
            The crucified Christ

He, then, becomes the air we breathe
He, then, becomes the beat of our hearts
He, then, becomes our first conscious thought when we awake and
the last prayer on our lips as we slip into sleep.

He was, He is and He will always be, our everything.
Amen.

...I am crucified with Christ, nevertheless I
        live, yet not I but Christ lives in me
and the life I now live, I live by the faith of the
        Son of God that loved me and gave
            himself for me. —The Apostle Paul
                Galatians 2:20

...In Him we live and move and have our
        being...—The Apostle Paul
            Acts 17:28

So often churchology insists receiving Jesus be a non-emo-
tional "decision." We are encouraged to walk an aisle, say a prayer
and perhaps fill out a card. People, other churchology members, con-
gratulate us and shake our hands. Then we are expected to immerse
ourselves in the life of the building: meetings, meals, gatherings,
teachings, and offerings.

I have found that after churchology there is Jesus. He reveals
Himself as the Father draws us. He comes when our hearts are empty
and our souls languishing from the crushing weight of sin. He comes.
He fixes. He fills us with joy unspeakable and full of glory! It is in this

context that we serve Him and serve others. Apart from Him we can do nothing, but with Him all things are possible. Amen.

Prayer:

Father in heaven,
Finding You is eternal life. Thank You
that You have promised that if
we seek You with all our hearts, You will let
us find You. Thank You that You
have not left us as orphans but have put
Your Spirit within us that cries out
"Abba, Father." We love you.
In the name of Jesus who fills us with joy, we pray,
Amen.

My Personal Reflections

_____

_____

_____

_____

_____

_____

_____

Perseverance 15

Through the valley
Dimly lit or up the mountain slope
All my steps are His to plot with
Graciousness and hope

      The path is seldom easy, the
      Way is strewn with fear
      But He is ever with me
      Perfecting all that I hold dear

            Slowly trudging up the mount
            Or running on the plain
            Life is an adventure, sometimes
            Crazy, sometimes sane

Embracing even dark clouds
Reaching for the moon
Certain of His watchful care
And that He's coming soon

      Often weary from the strain
      Or bludgeoned from behind
      Comforted by His strong arms
      His words so sweet, so kind

The battle rages, swords are drawn
The enemy is near
Legions for us gather round
The victory shout to hear

"Carry on, O, faithful one
Turn not left or right
Reward is certain for the saint
That continues in the night

We must not falter or turn aside
Let complaining cease
His blood has purchased all we need
Surrender and release."

Amen.

...Consider him who endured such opposition
from sinners, so that you will not
grow weary and lose heart.
In your struggle against sin, you have not yet
resisted to the point of shedding
your blood.—The writer of the Book of Hebrews
Hebrews 12:3-4

...Three times I was beaten with rods, once
I was stoned, three times I was
shipwrecked, a night and a day I have
spent in the deep. *I have been* on
frequent journeys, in dangers from rivers,
dangers from robbers, dangers
from *my* countrymen, dangers from the Gentiles,
dangers in the city, dangers in

the wilderness, dangers on the sea, dangers
among false brethren; *I have
been* in labor and hardship, through many
sleepless nights, in hunger and
thirst, often without food, in cold and exposure.—The Apostle Paul
2 Cor. 11:25–27

WHEN WE FIRST FELL in love with Jesus we probably did not fathom the depth of our life's response. We could not. At that point it was truly about His merciful arms and tender forgiveness. It was the glorious cleansing power of His blood that created a new heart in our bosoms and set our feet upon the paths of righteousness. It was the mighty wind of the Holy Spirit blowing away the dark clouds of destruction in order that the light of glory could cascade upon our souls. Do you remember?

Later, when the path becomes stony and His face becomes obscured by fierce storm clouds, then we stop to ponder. All forward motion comes to a halt as we find ourselves at the crossroads of pain and passion. Shall we press on? Is there yet another path? Perhaps a traverse less steep, less cruel, and less demanding.

It is at this juncture that injury and injustice rob the kingdom of many a jurist.

"He would not demand this of me. And if He does I no longer desire to participate." End of journey.

John 6:66 states: "From this time many of His disciples went back and no longer followed him." Did you notice the reference number? John 6:66. Six is the number of man; 666 the number of the Anti-christ, denying the Lord is the crux of the beast system. And so the Lord would also ask us today, as he responded to the disciples that remained, "Will you also go away?" Amen.

Prayer:

Faithful Father,
Forgive our wondering hearts when the
fire seeks to consume our faith.
Strengthen our resolve with Your ever-present Spirit. May
we set our faces as flint to forward motion. And may
we arrive safely at our pre-appointed destinations.
In the name of pilgrim Jesus, Your only Son,
Amen.

My Personal Reflections

_____
_____
_____
_____
_____
_____
_____

SERVANTHOOD 16

To lose is to gain in the kingdom of God
A dichotomy juxtaposed----strange and odd

To rejoice when
Reviled welcomes the King
A pride killing song that the heart stoops to sing

A solitary soul in the world of pain while
His presence comforts and prepares us to reign

Rising to serve, following His lead
The secret life hidden bearing fruit from the seed

To lose is to gain in the kingdom of God
A dichotomy juxtaposed—strange and odd.

…But Jesus called them to Himself and
said, "You know that the rulers of the
Gentiles lord it over them, and *their* great
men exercise authority over them. It
is not this way among you, but whoever wishes
to become great among you shall
be your servant, and whoever wishes to be
first among you shall be your
slave;—Jesus Christ
Matthew 20:25–27

...The first shall be last and the last shall be first.—Jesus Christ
Matthew 20:16

THE LESSONS OF THE kingdom are hard to learn; mainly because they go counter to the lessons the world teaches us: "Promote yourself." "The squeaky wheel gets the grease." "Dress to impress." In the kingdom, however, promotion comes to the ones that humble themselves under the mighty hand of God and await His time table of honor.

In the kingdom it is the meek that inherit the earth and silence is often required not discouraged. In the kingdom it is the robe of righteousness that identifies us as followers of Christ not the flash and bling of the adorning of the outward man. It is not easy to "unlearn" the ways of man and embrace the ways of the Spirit, but it will be eternally rewarding. Echoing the words of an old gospel song: It will be worth it all, when we see Jesus. Amen.

Prayer:

Heavenly Father,
We want to learn Your ways, not the ways of the
world. Purify our hearts and point us to the paths of
righteousness by the power of Your Eternal Spirit.
Give us an undivided heart that we may serve You perfectly.
In the precious name of Jesus, we pray,
Amen.

My Personal Reflections

Contentment 17

I saw it in the light of the sun's rays this morning:
Hope
Confidence coursing through the consciousness
of what is not, but in what shall be.

I felt it in the north breeze
Gently pushing summer into autumn:
Change arriving
Encouraged by the express expectations of eternity enduring.

I tasted it in the sweetness of the honeysuckle
that cascades down the broken
Branches of the backyard birch:
Happiness
Not with circumstances but with the Spirit's
urging to cast off discontent and
Determine to declare the defeat of that dastardly deceiver.

I heard it in the marvelous melody of the morning mockingbird:
Contentment
Blessed assurance that all He has promised
will produce the peace that
Permeates the present.

I smelled it in the aroma of the absolutely
amazing azaleas that graciously
Yield their precious perfume in perpetuity:
Consistency

Called to face the fiery trials with fierce fortitude from our
Father ever faithful.

I perceived it by the presence of His Holy Spirit
patiently waiting with persistent passion:
Indwelling
The godhead eternal taking up residency in the
beautiful blood bought bodies of every believer.

...For what can be known about God is plain
to them, because God has shown it
to them. For his invisible attributes, namely,
his eternal power and divine
nature, have been clearly perceived, ever since
the creation of the world, in the
things that have been made. So they are without excuse.
—The Apostle Paul
Romans 1:19–20

...The earth is the Lord's and the fullness
thereof the world and they that dwell
therein. He has founded it upon the waters
and established it upon the seas.—
King David
Psalm 24:1–2

THERE IS MUCH TO be said for contentment. It soothes the discontent of what-might-have been. It buoys the struggling believer and pacifies the perturbed. Just to count the blessings already given and rest in the satisfaction of knowing the giver of all things is on our side constitutes contentment.

It is truly the opposite of the world's ideology. The common curse of discontentment comes carried on the wings of every commercial.

We are bombarded with advertisers admonishing us to avert content-
ment; we must have the latest vehicle, the bigger home, and the newest
fashion. And once we attain what we thought would make us happy
we realize we must begin the cycle all over again: discontentment.

Looking beyond the lucre driven status symbols, however, we
find a world of wonder: the sun, the moon, the stars, the trees, the
flowers, and the birds. All of nature points us to His passion and our
true possessions. The scriptures tell us that He has freely given us all
things richly to enjoy. And while some think financial gain is godli-
ness, the truth is: godliness with contentment is great gain (1 Timothy
6:6). May we be content today in our salvation and every good and
perfect gift that comes down from above from the Father of light.

Amen.

Prayer:

Heavenly Father,
Thank You that all the universe declares Your glory. Please open our
hearts and minds to comprehend the wonder
of creation. We stand in awe of how
great Your works are and that we are part of Your divine
blueprint for all eternity. We worship Your majesty and
are grateful for the glorious display of Your genius.
In the name of Jesus, our contentment,
Amen.

My Personal Reflections

_____

_____

_____

_____

_____

_____

_____

PERSECUTION 18

It came to me to follow Christ, to make my life His own
I never stopped to wonder if the path be mud or stone
He called to me and beckoned on, as if I needed aid
To stay upon the thorny path that offered little shade
It hurt my feet and tore my flesh, no leniency received
The test of life required my heart to guard what it believed
Pushing, pushing up the mount weary without drink
If I should stop or turn around, my soul would surely sink
The night grew darker, pressing in, I longed to see the light
Struggling hard against the wind with doubt the cruelest blight
I tried to sing a sacred song, to lift my voice in praise
But sore the sound that served my lips was swallowed by the haze
Finally a hollow spot carved in the mountain's face
I turned inside the sheltered stone and cried for saving grace
It did not come by thunder blasts, nor lightning flashes seen
But deep within the mountain's breast, a voice both small and keen
"I promised tribulation with overcoming peace
To all that call upon my name from death a sure release
You are not journeying alone, My Spirit lifts your soul
And if you can but see My face true life as I've foretold"
I fell beneath His weighty words, I wept to feel him bend
So gently lifting me above the crushing curse of sin
Embraced by powers not my own, I turned to face the day
No longer burdened by defeat but courageous in the fray
Counting gain all but loss, seeking nothing more
His presence sweet with confidence His truth dispelling lore

And If I should die before I wake upon the celestial shores
His crimson blood will grant me life and open heaven's door.

…I am with you always, even unto the
end of the age.—Jesus Christ
Matthew 28:20

…In this world you will have tribulation, but
be of good cheer for I have overcome
the world.—Jesus Christ
John 16:33

FOR THE MOST PART, serving Jesus in America does not entail carrying a heavy burden. Not like Iraq, where five year old boys are being crucified, by a terror group known as ISIS, for clinging to the name of Jesus. Not like the Sudan where Christian churches are regularly burned and the women sold as sex slaves. Not like parts of Asia where the only approved form of worshipping Jesus is found "underground."

Perhaps, however, the winds of persecution are starting to blow from East to West. We seem to be reaping the seeds of government banned prayers in school and the abolishment of Bible studies in secular academia. We may be standing on the brink of participating with our brethren worldwide in bearing the reproach of Christ for our faith. Will the furnace of persecution be what purifies the Western Church? Will the faith of the faithful remain when the fire frequents our houses of prayer? Let us settle the issue in our hearts before the crisis arrives, denying the Lord is not an option. Even so, come quickly Lord Jesus.

Amen.

Prayer:

Father in heaven,
Focus our attention on Your provision and not on our
pain. Remind us precious Holy Spirit, that this world
is not our home. We are pilgrims only passing through.
Strengthen us to remain true to You at all costs.
Thank You that whatever we endure on this
earth is for our eternal well-being.
In the powerful name of Jesus who was also persecuted,
Amen.

My Personal Reflections

_____
_____
_____
_____
_____
_____
_____

THE FUTURE 19

My prayer:
"Father, help me understand and give me wisdom concerning the days we are now in."

His answer:
"I am not far from you
Nor distant from your cries-
I am the way the truth the life
Believe in me and never die

> Rest in my presence
> Drink from my cup
> Live in my Spirit
> Castings eyes always up

> I am your portion
> I am your song
> I am your direction
> In me is no wrong

> Seize the moment
> Cry out do not wait
> Now is forever
> Today is the date

CATHERINE ELAINE McPHERSON

Time is now standing
Apart from my plan
No man can manipulate
The course for this land

What I have started
I now will complete
Look to the skies
For the conclusion you'll meet

I am still speaking
Not all hear my voice
To be still and listen
Has become the great choice

My word will not falter
It stands high above
The deceiving voices
That speak only "love"

Those that I love
Are disciplined oft
You cannot ignore
That which I've taught

To obey is better
Than sacrifice brought
Adhere to the scriptures
And do as you ought

Do not fear what
Tomorrow may bring
Stay close to my heart
And let your soul sing

MY ALABASTER BOX...

I'm coming soon
For all that adhere
The blood of the lamb
Still draws Me near

On the door of your heart
The crimson red stain
Observed by the legions
As you continue to pray

Lean on my breast
Incline now your ear
Rejoice in my life
That you must hold dear

Lift up your head
Provisions been made
The kingdom is yours
The debt has been paid

Do not lose sight
And do not grow weary
The race will be won
By the brave not the leery

Cast all your crowns
At my feet and rejoice
My shield is your portion
Protecting your choice

As the darkness looms close
And evil more bold
Stay under my wings
As the story unfolds

I will not desert you
I cannot fail
What is written is coming
To my wind lift your sail---"

Selah.

⁓⁓⁓⁓

...Heaven and earth will pass away but my Word
will never pass away.—Jesus Christ
Matthew 24:35

...The Lord Almighty has sworn, "Surely, as
I have planned, so it will be, and as
I have purposed, so it will happen.
Isaiah 14:24

MANY PROPHETIC WORDS ARE blowing in the wind. You can find a "word from the Lord" to match your personal beliefs on almost any subject. End times teachings are no exception. From belief in the imminent return of Christ to church planners projecting into the next one hundred years, there is a plethora of prophecies from which the public may partake.

But truly, does it not really come down to hearing the voice of the Lord for ourselves? It absolutely does not profit us to hear from man if we cannot correctly discern the voice of the Father. If we are listening to tales of end-times scenarios that are opposite the holy scriptures, we better beware! We must only embrace prophecies that reflect what is written in the Bible. As Jesus said, "Be careful how you hear."

Amen.

Prayer:

Heavenly Father,
We thank You for sending the Holy Spirit to lead us
into all truth and show us things to come. Thank You
that Your Spirit and Your Word will always agree.
Give us discernment as we live out the closing days of this age.
In the name of Jesus, the eternal Son of God,
Amen.

My Personal Reflections

_____

_____

_____

_____

_____

_____

_____

*D*ETERMINATION 20

I gladly give my life to you
Your holiness, your grace
Where unexpected pleasures come
Within the heated race

What hinders me?
The world of tests: erratic feelings pour
Unchecked from deep within my breast
Like sirens soft with lore

I trip, I fall, I rise again
To offer you my best
Your love besets my brokenness
To offer grace and rest

I gladly give my life to You
Your perfect light and life
Your presence pure secures my peace
From darkness, pain and strife

I shan't turn back
Or slack my stride
Though climbing higher still
I'll stay the course undaunted
'Til my heart becomes Thy will

...Although I want to do good, evil is right
there with me. For in my inner being I
delight in God's Law; but I see another law at
work in me, waging war against the
law of my mind and making me a prisoner
of the law of sin at work within me.
What a wretched man I am! Who will rescue
me from this body that is subject to
death? Thanks be to God, who delivers me through
Jesus Christ our Lord!—The Apostle Paul
Romans 7:21–25

...And it came to pass, when the time was
come that he should be received up,
he [Jesus] steadfastly set his face to go to
Jerusalem.—Luke the Physician
Gospel of Luke 9:51

AS WE WALK THROUGH this world we are offered many opportunities to live distracted from the Lord's purposes. There is the distraction of work, of home, of family, of friends. There is the distraction of entertainment, sports, hobbies, and activities both secular and religious. None of these things listed are evil in and of themselves, however they are constantly screaming for our undivided attention, drowning out that which is sacred and holy. Distractions easily become what determines our direction and deflects us from what is needful for the kingdom of heaven. Yes, we live in the world but we are not *of this world*. We must set our heart on the things of the Lord with a determined diligence that defies the devil; the Lord and His kingdom must be first. Amen.

Prayer:

Father in heaven,
We are so grateful that when we fall down, You pick us
up and put our feet back on the correct path. Thank
You that we have the power to persevere through Your
precious Spirit. Keep us in Your love as we set our faces
like flint to find ourselves in the New Jerusalem.
We pray in the name of the way, the truth and the life, Jesus Christ,
Amen.

My Personal Reflections

_____

_____

_____

_____

_____

_____

BETRAYAL 21

How frail the flower
Whose head is turned
By but a whispered chant

What the weakness
Now unseen that
Wilts the tender plant?

And is it yet a travesty
The silent wind
Of fate

That draws the
Life of daffodils
From morning dawn to late

The beauty of the petals
Gone before the
Gale wind wept

Her face has dropped
Returned to earth
The promise yet unkept.

...For no sooner has the sun risen with a
burning heat than it withers the grass;
its flower falls and its beautiful appearance
perishes.—The Apostle James
James 1:11

...Trust ye not in a friend, put ye not confidence
in a guide; keep the doors of thy
mouth from her that lieth in thy bosom—The Prophet Micah
Micah 7:5

IT IS THE PERSON unusual that lives life outside the boundaries of betrayal. Few will walk unscathed by broken covenants or unprofitable promises. It is truly part and parcel of participating in the human dilemma. Because we all are born under the curse of original sin, the consequences are more than we can fathom; unfaithful words are one of them.

We tried to solve this problem early on by making our childhood friends issue pinkie promises, crossing our hearts hoping to die, or even becoming joined in a blood-brother covenant by mingling each other's blood after scratching our wrists with a sharp rock. None of it worked. We still found ourselves rejected by our buddies, alone on the playground, or the brunt of secrets spread through the closeted cliques.

Then we grew up. We were surprised, but not altogether naïve with the deception so prevalent in the adult theatre. Perhaps, we not only were recipients but perpetrators of misspoken words as well. Maneuvering through such experiences is neither easy nor pleasant, but one that in many ways will shape the years following the damage of deceit.

Becoming wiser from such an ordeal involves forgiveness as well as repentance. Forgiving the one who failed us. And repenting for our own participation: blindly placing our hearts in the hands of men instead of the Lord. Trust must be measured in the context of our dependence on the Father first and men second. If we reverse the order we are in trouble.

Even with the best intentioned words of commitment, life happens. It is in this moment that we must find the supernatural assurance of the Father's faithfulness. He is the only one that can absolutely and eternally keep His promise, for underneath are the everlasting arms; even when we are unfaithful, He remains faithful. Amen.

Prayer:

Father in heaven,
We thank You that when we are unfaithful, You
remain faithful. You cannot deny Yourself.
Help us, Lord, to keep covenant with those with whom
we have been joined. Help us by Your Holy Spirit to
remain true to promises made and contracts signed.
Give us a forgiving heart toward those who have failed us.
We encourage ourselves with the knowledge that our hope
is in the name of the Lord who made heaven and earth.
In the faithful name of Jesus,
Amen.

My Personal Reflections

_____

_____

_____

_____

_____

_____

_____

FAMILY DIVISION

22

I drank from the cup
She gave me, my sister,
Not too long ago

I held the cup in both
My hands and wished
Her heart to know

To see her smile
To talk with her, to laugh
And cry and share

In oneness drive
Away the angry cloud
That cancelled out the care

Its work well done
The silence thick, it
Smothered every hope

Of change and peace
Such disregard is hard
To bear and cope

Against my soul
Like a pleading child,
Locked out in the dark of night

Crying in the cold
Without a voice
Without a claim in sight

Oh, that reconciliation
Were the deed and not
Just such a word

That hearts again could
Share the light that
Makes ridicule absurd

I cannot bring what
Was to now, nor force
A mind to bend

My only recourse
I find in prayer
The one who understands

The comfort of my Lord
Who came and
Suffered for my care

I call to you, O Jesus,
Blow the clouds away
And take the load I bear

...Where there is strife, there is pride, but wisdom
is found in those who take advice.
—King Solomon
Proverbs 13:10

...He heals the brokenhearted and binds
up their wounds—King David
Psalm 147:3

BEING ALIENATED FROM A brother or sister is true anguish; especially when the separation comes from the heart of the offended and not your own. Regardless of the root, the void remains resonant as long as silence prevails where there was once patronage.

Prayer and time and then time and prayer; sometimes, more prayer and more time. Both pass slowly when calls go unanswered and emails are blocked. Navigating through the waves of broken siblinghood is a balancing act. We must respect the boundaries drawn and at the same time not grow accustomed to the distance divided. It is not easy.

The Word commands us to be at peace with all as far as it is possible. Finding peace in the broken communion is only possible with Christ. It is found in casting all our cares upon Him and believing that He will make all things beautiful in His time. It is His promise. Amen.

Prayer:

Father in heaven,
When the enemy comes to separate, divide, and destroy, You
have promised to lift up a standard against him. You who have
reconciled all mankind to Yourself through the shed blood of
Jesus Christ desire that we be reconciled one to another. Have
Your way, Father, in our families both now and forever,
In the name of Jesus, the great reconciler,
Amen.

My Personal Reflections

_____

_____

_____

MY ALABASTER BOX...

_____

_____

_____

_____

CREATION

23

A December rose bloomed
In my yard
A testimony of grace
Its petals damp with winter's rain
Embroidered as with lace.

⁓⁓⁓

...For since the creation of the world God's
invisible qualities-his eternal power
and divine nature-have been clearly seen, being
understood from what has been
made, so that people are without excuse.—The Apostle Paul
Romans 1:20

...How many are your works, O, Lord! In
wisdom you made them all; the earth
is full of Your creatures!—King David
Psalms 104:24

IT IS ABSOLUTELY AMAZING when nature defies the seasons to display the glory of its Creator. Roses are not supposed to bloom in the winter, but when they do a clear message is manifested. The One who creates does as He will and delivers His divine signature to mankind: "Everything is in my hand and I determine the times and the seasons for all things."

Resting in His great design is comforting as well as awe-inspiring. Nothing is hid from Him and nothing is forgotten by Him. No one is an accident and every living thing is purposefully positioned on planet Earth at His bidding and for His pleasure. Even the December rose.

Amen.

Prayer:

Heavenly Father,
We worship You for Your omnipotence. We worship You for Your watchful care over all of creation. We are thankful that all the earth and its inhabitants indicate Your infinite intelligence.
We stand in awe of You.
In the awe-inspiring name of Jesus Christ, Your Son,
Amen.

My Personal Reflections

_____

_____

_____

_____

_____

_____

_____

CONFUSION

24

I never thought I'd
Walk this path
A twisting road not chosen

Where light has dimmed
And truth is skewed
And natural affections frozen

The ideas embraced
Are not mine
Trespassers, cold foreboding

Imposters all
In shadows grow
True honor now withholding

The path is steep
It yields no pause
Demanding strength to journey

Pressed from behind
By birds of prey
To stop, to sigh, forlornly

I want again
The pasture green
Where truth springs fresh eternal

MY ALABASTER BOX...

Where streams are clear
And air to breathe
Traditions firm, paternal

Each tear I shed
Is not in vain
Each prayer a stone to pave

Though dimly lit
My footing sure
A soul to keep and save

Strength for today
My constant prayer
No turning from the fray

Rehearsing songs
Of victory,
Regaining those that stray

Walk beside me
Friend or foe
This path favors neither

I will not
Doubt the end result
That stands beyond the ether

I will rejoice
In heaven's balm
The blood bought and the certain

A Father true
That strides with me
Beyond the veil, the curtain

Press on, press on
O Pilgrim heart
Let truth your candle be

Till darkness dies
Consumed by light
And righteousness decreed

...My tears have been my bread day and night.
While they continually say to me
"Where is your God?"—King David
Psalm 42:3

...Oh, send out Your light and Your truth! Let
them lead me. Let them bring me
to Your holy hill, and to Your tabernacle.
Then will I go to the altar of God to
God my exceeding joy; And on the harp I will
praise you, O God, my God.—King David
Psalm 43:3–4

PERHAPS, THE GREATEST DISAPPOINTMENTS in life are connected to our off-spring; our seed. Is it not natural for a parent to desire that their prodigy present themselves in a manner deemed worthy of the name they carry? Certainly the hopes and dreams of the paternal include the passing on to the children the values, attitudes and faith of the ones that gave them life in the first place. It is only natural.

But, the unnatural occurs all too often. We could call it a mutation of sorts. When the child morphs into someone undistinguishable from the understood and preplanned. The struggle that ensues is enormous. The tension between love and rejection becomes tremendous. We struggle to make sense of a reality we never asked for nor did we see coming. We have decisions to make.

Are we able to love the sinner and hate the sin? Is the mantra "love wins" even applicable? What does that even mean? Which love? What kind of love? Are we required to obey scriptural mandates that in turn may alienate our children?

There are no easy answers. However, for the parent that refuses to be politically correct, and for the mother or father that has decided to cling to scripture over progressive religious agendas, the answer can be found. There is to be no compromise with the covenant. There is no watering down of the Word of Yahweh. Jesus stated plainly, If you love mother or father or sons or daughters more than me you are not worthy of me. When we find ourselves in a position of choice, may we have the courage to choose the Lord's way over the world's way. It is the right way. And as we stand for His truth, He has promised to contend with those that contend with us and to save our children. (Isaiah 49:25) Amen.

Prayer:

Heavenly Father,
Prepare our hearts for the unexpected. Fashion truth
in our innermost being, so when challenged by
the untruth, we cling to that which is holy.
Sustain within us the steadfast love of the Lord that never
changes, and the confidence that all things work together for
good to those who love the Lord and are called according to
His purpose. Thanking You, Father, that You will never fail.
In the name of your perfect son, Jesus Christ,
Amen.

My Personal Reflections

_____
_____
_____
_____
_____

THE BLOOD OF JESUS 25

So strong the blood that stems the flood of Satan's spurious schemes
So sweet the taste the victor's race in heaven's glorious streams
No power can stand, no demon band against the crimson tide
No enemy's blow nor dark forebode when Jesus does abide
Ho! Now Pilgrim all eyes on Him, run strong into the night
Ho! Believer cease not ever embracing truth and light
The victor's crown goes not to him who says he has
Prevailed, but to him who humbly bows
Beneath the cross-torn veil.

...Therefore brethren, since we have confidence
to enter the holy place by the
blood of Jesus, by a new and living way, which
He inaugurated for us through the
veil, that is His flesh, and since we have a great
priest over the house of God, let
us draw near with a sincere heart in full
assurance of faith, having our hearts
sprinkled clean from an evil conscience and our bodies
washed with pure water.—The Writer of Hebrews
Hebrews 10:19–22

...And they sang a new song, saying, "Worthy
are You to take the book and to

break its seals; for You were slain, and purchased
for God with Your blood men
from every tribe and tongue and people and
nation. You have made them to be
a kingdom of priests to our God and they will
reign upon the earth.—John the Revelator
Revelations 5:9–10

THE WORD OF GOD has much to say about the blood of Jesus. The current church, however, not so much. The old hymns declaring the wondrous works of that crimson tide are rarely resurrected on a typical Sunday morning. Songs like "Nothing But the Blood of Jesus," "Are You Washed in The Blood?" "Covered by the Blood," "There Is a Fountain Filled With Blood," "There is Power in the Blood." Where have these songs gone? Has the Church become a bloodless body?

As the songs have changed so have the sermons. Few pastors spend time instructing their parishioners on the privileges of pleading the blood of Jesus. How long has it been since we have been encouraged to meditate on the immeasurable benefits of His blessed and holy blood? And when was the last time we were served the body and the blood of Jesus in the Holy Sacrament as a blessed memorial to His sacrifice.

The natural body is dead without blood; we simply cease to exist if we lose our blood. Our spiritual bodies are likewise affected. A blood-less church is a powerless church. A blood-less church cannot withstand the satanic onslaught of this age. There is power in the blood, wonder working power. Let us embrace it and seek its provision both now and forever. Amen.

Prayer:

Father in heaven,
Forgive us for allowing the blood of Your Son
to become obsolete in the church.
We repent for becoming indifferent to our
identity crisis without its presence.
Help us understand that we must fully embrace the
blood of Jesus, for therein lies our salvation.
In the name of the only One that gave His
lifeblood for mankind, Jesus Christ,
Amen.

My Personal Reflections

_____
_____
_____
_____
_____
_____
_____

OBEDIENCE

26

I took the desert moon with me
And placed it in my heart
And even though I felt its glow
I knew it would depart

I struggled hard to justify
My claim upon its light
But the Creator's song rang out
Capturing the night

And so the moon shines brightly still
Back amongst the stars
Securely fixed and hung in space
Safe beyond the bar

My heart much wiser though less bright
Agrees with times decreed
Relinquishing all claims that own
The sower and the seed

The Light that made the light
And gave it strength to shine
Now beckons me to higher heights
Communion and to dine

Expectant souls reach out in truth
To worship and comply

Resisting every shadowy gift
That to the earth would tie

And what the cost to life or limb
And what the sacrifice?
But echoes even deeper love
Of cross and blood entice

Always in the eastern sky
The silvery buoyant orb
Reminding me that Christ demands
That eagles rise and soar

...Seek ye first the Kingdom of God and His
righteousness and all these things
shall be added unto you.—Jesus Christ
Matthew 6:33

...What does it profit a man if he gain the whole
world and lose his soul?—Jesus Christ
Mark 8:36

As BELIEVERS, IF WE make anything more important than the kingdom of God and His righteousness we are on shaky ground. Even doing the "ministry" can become an extra curricular activity that consumes our passion for the person of Jesus Christ. We are called to make the main thing, the main thing.

What is the main thing? Remember, the sibling group Mary, Martha and Lazarus? They were close friends of the Lord's and the scriptures tell us that Jesus spent much time in their home when He was in Bethany. Martha may have been the oldest as she seemed to be the take charge and get it done, type A personality. She also was the most vocal. She complained loudly to the Lord about her sister sitting at His feet, lost in the beauty of His holiness, while she slaved away in the kitchen. She asked Jesus to tell Mary to get up and help her.

Jesus may have seemed unsympathetic to her request with his response. However, He was all about establishing truth and kingdom principles. Jesus countered her complaint with the following: "Martha, Martha, you are busy and encumbered about with many things, Mary has chosen the best and it will not be taken from her." Mary chose the "best."

The "best" is being with the Lord. The "best" is listening for His voice and hearing His voice. The "best" is receiving from His hand every good and perfect gift. We must understand that activity born outside of being with Him is just that: activity. The "best" is allowing him to preorder our paths and designate our daily assignments. It is all about receiving our responsibilities from relationship. The "best" springs from being with Jesus. Amen.

Prayer:

Heavenly Father,
Draw us to yourself by Your wonderful Holy Spirit. Open our eyes to see the beauty of being in Your presence. Give us understanding to the power of sitting still at Your feet. We have come into Your kingdom to do Your good pleasure. We pray in the name above all names, Jesus the Christ, Amen.

My Personal Reflections

_____
_____
_____
_____
_____
_____
_____

Written in honor of my Dad, Henry F. McCabe, on his ninety fourth birthday.

Like a lighthouse to a sailor on a stormy sea
Like a bright beam to a pilot fighting hard to see
Like a friendly flag to a refugee
Like a flickering flame to a floundering me

Your light has held steady
Shining strong constantly
A blessing to many
But especially me

…Let your light so shine among men that
they see your good works and glorify
your Father which is in heaven.—Jesus Christ
Matthew 5:15

…Ye are the light of the world. A city set on
a hill cannot be hid.—Jesus Christ
Matthew 5:14

WE ARE TOLD THAT in many ways our earthly father predisposes us to either love our heavenly Father or to run away from Him. If our earthly father treated us kindly we have no problem seeing Father

God as a good and benevolent deity. However, if our earthly father was a tyrant, that is often the way we perceive the Father in heaven and we respond accordingly.

Fathers who protect and esteem their children are paving a pathway to the one true God, Yahweh. For those are His attributes as reflected in the scriptures:

"I will be a shelter for you, a strong tower from your enemies," and "I will be with you in time of trouble, I will deliver you and honor you."(Psalms 61:3, Psalms 91:15)

Faithful, covenant keeping fathers make it easy for their children to relate to a heavenly Father that will never leave them nor forsake them. Unfortunately the opposite is also true. The dead beat dad that forsakes his parenting responsibilities put their off spring in a precarious spiritual position. If the child cannot trust the father that they can see, how are they to trust the Father that they cannot see.

If our earthly father set the right example, let us give thanks today. Certainly, we will not find the perfect earthly father, but the one that lays down his own desires and truly tries to walk godly before his children is to be honored and esteemed. They are a rare breed and we should give honor to whom honor is due. However, if our earthly fathers did not set the right example, may we find the grace and goodwill to forgive them. And may we renew our covenant with our Father in heaven to rightly represent Him to our own children. Amen.

Prayer:

Our Father in heaven,
Thank You for the gift of earthly fathers. We ask that the words of
Malachi the prophet be manifest in our days: I will turn the hearts
of the fathers back to the children and the hearts of the children
back to the fathers, lest I come and smite the earth with a curse.
In the name of the only begotten of the Father, Jesus our Lord,
Amen.

My Personal Reflections

_____

_____

_____

_____

_____

_____

*D*ISCIPLESHIP
28

To know and to be known by life in the Spirit
To contemplate earth's journey and to truly live it

To flow like a river as He turns the tide
To be overshadowed in His love and there to abide

To give Him all glory, to praise His great name
To understand Jesus and God are the same

To yearn for His presence and His embrace
To follow His lead and to seek
His sweet face

There's no higher calling
No service as great
As before Him falling
A disciple's true trait

…Jesus said unto him, Thomas, because thou
hast seen me, thou hast believed:
blessed are they that have not seen, and
yet have believed.—Jesus Christ
John 20:29

¹⁷ ...And when I saw him, I fell at his feet as dead.
And he laid his right hand upon me, saying unto
me, Fear not; I am the first and the last:
I am he that lives, and was dead; and, behold,
I am alive for evermore, Amen;
and have the keys of hell and of death.—Jesus Christ

Revelation 1:17–18

WHAT IS THE GOAL of the modern day disciple? Should it be any different than the desire of the 1st century disciple? Knowing Him, loving Him, worshipping Him and obeying Him should all be at the top of the list. What's not to love about Him? What relationship could complete us like the Christ's? Is there any other life force that could possibly fill that god-shaped vacuum in our hearts?

When Jesus spoke the hard truth of true discipleship, many of his adherents went away and followed Him no more. The Lord turned to the hand-picked twelve and gave them an opportunity at mutiny too: "Do you want to leave me also?"

Peter's reply still resonates: "Where would we go Lord, only You have the words of eternal life." Amen.

Prayer:

Father in heaven,
We worship You, the one true God. We are thankful that You
have revealed Yourself through Jesus Christ, your only Son.
May we be single-minded in our devotion
to our Savior and His kingdom.
May we bask in Your presence and find contentment
in His covenant. May our hearts be totally captured
by the courage and confidence of Christ.
In the name of Jesus our King,
Amen.

My Personal Reflections

_____

_____

_____

_____

_____

_____

_____

DIRECTION 29

Sonnet 1

Seeking the truth, following after it hard
Determined to win come hell or sharp barb
Risking it all, playing wisely each card
Warrior ready, dressed-out in the garb

Undaunted in spirit, racing ahead
Zealous in soul, running each show
Lost in persuasion or intentionally misled
Resisting all pressure, we go with the flow

But God will be God, He will not relent
Though circumstances odd, human efforts all spent
We plan and perform till the Lord's perfect storm
Live through the disaster and buffet the norm

He breaks through the pain with His perfect call
Responding to humans the weak and the small

...For I can testify about them that they are
zealous for God, but their zeal is not
based on knowledge.—The Apostle Paul
Romans 10:2

Just as a father has compassion on *his* children,

So the Lord has compassion on those who fear Him.
For He Himself knows our frame;
He is mindful that we are *but* dust.—King David
Psalms 103:13–14

BEING ZEALOUS IS NOT sufficient. We can be gung-ho and horribly wrong at the same time. We may find ourselves sincerely planted in our own purposes and not the purpose of the Lord. The Father does not wring His hands. His commitment does not wane with our wrong understanding of His perfect will. He speaks again, His desire to delineate and patiently waits for our deafness to dissipate. And should we, out of ignorance or insolence, continue on the wrong path, He has the power and compassion to apply the necessary pressure to correct. Amen.

Prayer:

Father in heaven,
How awesome is Your love and commitment to us, Your children.
Thank You that You do not give up on us. Grant us tender
hearts to comply and spiritual ears that hear You loud
and clear. Enable us by Your Spirit to change directions
quickly and easily as You guide us to our expected end.
In the name of Jesus our example,
Amen.

My Personal Reflections

_____

_____

_____

_____

_____

_____

Sonnet 2

Tears of pain with anxiety fraught
Questioning fate, depression and what?
Trying to listen for lessons taught
Disdaining doubts, and groans so distraught

No answers to give, no wisdom displayed
Neither pseudo compassion nor sympathy feigned
No beautiful gowns so gloriously arrayed
Only weak arms that cannot sustain

But time does not stand still or retreat
It hastens to cadence unheard or observed
Deceiving us all to hold possessions complete
Displaying emotions raw and unnerved

Releasing all gall we must fall on our knees
To honor our Lord who answers our pleas

…When I expected good, then evil came;
When I waited for light, then darkness
came.—The Patriarch Job
Job 30:26

> ...Forgive us our trespasses as we forgive those
> who trespass against us.—Jesus Christ
> Matthew 6:12

CORRECTLY COPING WITH DISAPPOINTMENTS is crucial. For Christians and non-Christians alike offences often seem omnipresent. And thus, we find life is full of opportunities to forgive or not. Choosing the later opens the heart for what the scriptures refer to as a root of bitterness. Allowing such a root to grow bears a bitter fruit of resentment that becomes painfully apparent to all we come in contact with.

A true test of maturing in our faith is how fast we forgive. Do we linger in our justified injustice or are we quick to relinquish our pain to the one who pacifies all improprieties? And if we really want to measure our spirituality, are we able to forgive before the offender even asks for absolution? Our example prayed "Father, forgive them for they know not what they are doing." He sets the bar high, but following His lead imparts peace and takes away the enemy's opportunity to oppress our souls. Forgiveness bears the fruit of sound sleep and good digestion. Think about it. Amen.

Prayer:

Father in heaven,
Grant us the grace to freely forgive even as Your Son
forgave those who crucified Him. Grant us courage to
bless those that curse us and to do good to those that
despitefully use us. May we rejoice in all things, knowing
nothing touches our lives without Your permission.
In the name of the Savior that forgives, Jesus the Christ,
Amen.

My Personal Reflections

_____
_____
_____
_____
_____
_____
_____

Sonnet 3

Grim reaper standing just at the door
Positioned silent against the night
Long arms outstretched and nothing more
Like a dark but luminous light

I think it is a smile I see
Perhaps his unrepentant grin
Whispering what might or might not be
He fakes them both the truth and sin

Ho! At the door he must concede
No further entrance gain
The God of light determines lead
The length of life and pain

Orchestrating from what seems afar
The crossing, the crossing, of the bar

...I am the Living One; I was dead, and now
look, I am alive for ever and ever!
And I hold the keys of death and Hades.—Jesus Christ
Revelation 1:28

...Therefore, since the children share in flesh
and blood, He Himself likewise also
partook of the same, that through death He
might render powerless him who had
the power of death, that is, the devil, and
might free those who through fear of
death were subject to slavery all their lives.—
The Writer of the Book of Hebrews
Hebrews 2:14–15

WATCHING A LOVED ONE die is a very traumatic event; even when death is expected. Powerless to stop the process our hearts are often divided between holding them to this earth and releasing them into eternity. We have not that grasp. It is, however, with confidence in the one that does that we find hope and comfort.

Death is described as the last enemy to be conquered. We understand that Jesus conquered death when He arose from the dead. We get it with our minds, but then the heart becomes over-ridingly involved as our dearest lies on the bed of death. It is in this moment that we desperately need faith to become sight.

It is true that death is our enemy. It is truer still that the Lord of life is also the Lord over death. As the scripture states, "It is appointed unto man once to die and after that the judgment." We all have our appointment and as with all appointments we must prepare.

Stepping across the bar will bring eternal pleasure in the presence of the Father or eternal torment separated from the Creator. The good news is that Jesus has made the way for those who choose Him as their Savior to be cleansed of their sins and presented holy to the one who dwells in the holy place. Embracing the blood of Jesus as our reconciliation brings redemption and the reward of heaven. Let us not neglect so great a salvation. Amen

Prayer:

Father in heaven,
Thank You that You have made provision for the living
and those that are not. Thank You that You are with us
in life and when our bodies are no longer alive. We place
our trust in Your eternal sacrifice to transport us safely
from this world to the next as we live our lives in You.
Thank You for all things seen and unseen.
In the blessed name of our guide across the bar, Jesus Christ,
Amen.

My Personal Reflections

_____
_____
_____
_____
_____
_____
_____

INDEX OF SCRIPTURES

\# 26   Matthew 6:33, Mark 8:36
\# 27   Matthew 5:15, Matthew 5:14
\# 28   John 20:29, Revelation 1:17–18
\# 29   Romans 10:2, Psalm 103:13–14
\# 30   Job 30:26, Matthew 6:12
\# 31   Revelation 1:28, Hebrews 2:14–15

ABOUT THE AUTHOR

THE TWISTS AND TURNS of life have provided Catherine with more than enough personal material for plenty of poems, endless journal entries, and a plethora of prayers. Being a wife of forty-seven years, a mother of seven children (four biological and three adopted), a state certified teacher, and an ordained minister have helped to season her poetry with truth and hope.

Catherine's diverse life experiences have influenced her writings with a unique blend of grace and obedience. Her life's passion is for others to come to faith in Jesus Christ and to love the Lord with all their heart, with all their soul, with all their strength and with all their mind. Amen.

CPSIA information can be obtained
at www.ICGtesting.com
Printed in the USA
BVHW03075710122l
623720BV00001B/6

9 781644 921081